MARCO ISLAND

Many people remember the first time they found Marco Island. Implicit in that assertion is an eventual return, whether as a vacationer, snowbird, or full-time resident. The island's unique charm practically sells itself, but during the past 50 years, it has been captured, branded, and amplified by ambitious developers, as pictured in this billboard. (Courtesy of the Marco Island Historical Society.)

ON THE FRONT COVER: A young family has a picnic on the beach at the Marco Beach Hotel & Villas in a c. 1967 Deltona Corporation promotional photograph. (Courtesy of the Marco Island Historical Society.)

UPPER BACK COVER: Guests arrive under the porte cochère at the Marco Beach Hotel & Villas in 1967. (Courtesy of the Marco Island Historical Society.)

LOWER BACK COVER (from left to right): The brand-new Marco River Bridge, opened in 1969, reduced the driving distance to Naples by 12 miles; people conveniently board the boat *Julo* from a backyard on Marco Island in 1968; a golfer tees off at the sixth hole in the sixth annual Tony Lema Memorial Tournament at the Marco Island Country Club in 1972. (All, courtesy of the Marco Island Historical Society.)

Images of Modern America

MARCO ISLAND

AUSTIN J. BELL, KAITLIN ROMEY, AND
THE MARCO ISLAND HISTORICAL SOCIETY

ARCADIA
PUBLISHING

Published by Arcadia Publishing
Charleston, South Carolina

Library of Congress Control Number: 2018952262

For all general information, please contact Arcadia Publishing:
Telephone 843-853-2070
Fax 843-853-0044
E-mail sales@arcadiapublishing.com
For customer service and orders:
Toll-Free 1-888-313-2665

Visit us on the Internet at www.arcadiapublishing.com

*In honor of Herb Savage and his immeasurable
impact on Marco Island and its history*

CONTENTS

ACKNOWLEDGMENTS

This book would not have been possible without the support of the Marco Island Historical Society (MIHS) and its board of directors. Many thanks to the supportive staff of the Marco Island Historical Museum (MIHM), including Nancy Judd, Jessica Patel, Susan Pernini, Jennifer Perry, and Patricia Rutledge. Thanks also go to the generous members and supporters of the MIHS, as well as the Marco Island community, to whom this book is primarily written.

The authors are grateful to the following for selflessly donating materials to the MIHS that now appear within the pages of this book: Janice Brewer, Diane Chestnut, Alice Herndon, Leonard Llewellyn, Valerie Maerker, Herbert R. Savage, Richard Teibel, Jim and Julie Wallace, Bruce Wessells, and the Marco Island Area Association of Realtors.

The authors also wish to acknowledge the following for granting permission to reproduce their images within the pages of this book: the Deltona Corporation, the *Marco Eagle*, *Reader's Digest*, the City of Marco Island, Smith Aerial Photography, Aerial Photography by Don & Roy Couture (1-800-317-8207), David Henderson (SunshineSkies.com), Mark Bahr (Bahr family archives), and Joey Waves (Island Media Group).

Craig Woodward deserves special mention and thanks for his edits as well as his endless contributions to the MIHS and the MIHM and for sharing Marco Island's history.

The authors are appreciative of Douglas Waitley and Michael Coleman, whose respective books *The Last Paradise: The Building of Marco Island* and *Marco Island: Florida's Gulf Playground* are two of the only published works on Marco Island's modern era.

Austin Bell wishes to acknowledge his wife, Erin Wolfe Bell; his parents, David and Linda Bell; and his sisters, Allison and Angela Bell, for encouraging and inspiring the pursuit of life's passions.

Kaitlin Romey wishes to thank her husband, Nate; parents, Mike and Cindy Manley; Kyle Manley; and Jenna Williamson for their constant support.

Unless otherwise noted, all images appear courtesy of the Marco Island Historical Society. All errors are the authors' own.

INTRODUCTION

It is easy to understand what first-time visitors to Marco Island find alluring about the sun-soaked tropical island in Florida's Gulf of Mexico. Googling Marco Island yields a dazzling array of idyllic images awash in tropical blues, greens, and whites. The sugar-sand beach, ocean breezes, swaying palm trees, and balmy temperatures have been drawing visitors to Marco Island's shores for decades.

Yet there is more to Marco Island than first meets the eye. Steeped in a remarkable history with residents bound by a common sense of identity, civic duty, and community pride, Marco Island is the kind of place that not only draws people to its shores but also convinces them to put down roots. Even so, life on a six-by-four-mile barrier island is not always lived without adversity. Perhaps what is most remarkable about Marco Island is the way in which its people have met and overcome a variety of challenges during the past 50 years.

On September 10, 2017, the unthinkable unfolded on Marco Island. Hurricane Irma, once a Category 5 hurricane in the Caribbean and one of the strongest Atlantic hurricanes ever observed, made a beeline for the 23-square-mile island. It had been 12 years since Hurricane Wilma, Marco Island's last major hurricane, and many newcomers had yet to experience anything remotely resembling Irma. Mandatory evacuations went into effect, leaving most of the island empty, with those choosing to stay hunkered down and preparing for the worst. Meteorologists predicted a 10- to 15-foot storm surge, and Marco Island became ground zero for an evolving national news story.

At about 2:30 p.m., Hurricane Irma made landfall at Marco Island as a Category 3 hurricane with sustained winds of 115 miles per hour. The Marco Island Police Department reported a wind gust of 130 miles per hour. The strong winds blew water out into the Gulf of Mexico, creating unusual sights and record low-water readings before the storm surge brought it all back (and then some) in a hurry. Mercifully, the dire surge predictions did not hold true, as the storm weakened just prior to arrival. In Goodland, a storm surge tide sensor measured a water level greater than seven feet, and the rest of Marco Island saw only three- to five-foot inundation above ground level.

Nevertheless, the destruction was extensive. Most of the buildings in nearby Everglades City suffered major damage. At least 88 buildings were destroyed in Collier County, and another 1,500 were badly damaged. There was heavy tree and power-pole damage on Marco Island, and nearly every roof suffered at least some harm. The island is still recovering as of this writing, and it will take years for the physical scars of the storm to completely disappear, barring another hurricane of similar magnitude. What many people will remember about Hurricane Irma, though, including the authors, is the way in which the community pulled together during and after the storm.

Countless people volunteered their time, energy, and money to the recovery efforts. Although many were dealing with their own problems large and small, they still pitched in to help their friends and neighbors. The storm even led to the formation of the Marco Patriots, a group of volunteer civilians that provided information and updates during and immediately after the storm, eventually raising almost $150,000 to aid hurricane relief. Marco Island was open for business again only months after the storm, just in time for its annual season.

After Hurricane Irma, the sense of community and pride in Marco Island was arguably as high as it had ever been. What was it about this place that made its people respond in the way that they did? How did so many generous and compassionate individuals find their way to Marco Island? From where did this strong sense of community originate? There are undoubtedly many answers to these questions, most of which lie in the individuals and their personal histories, but many are also rooted in decisions made more than 50 years ago, when the dream of developing Marco Island into a self-sufficient island community was still in its infancy.

In 1962, Florida's "Famous Mackle Brothers," a trio of real estate developers from Miami, visited Marco Island at the request of its then-majority landowners. The Mackles could not believe what they saw: a sparsely populated and pristine island paradise that could one day be home to thousands. Under the auspices of the Deltona Corporation, the Mackles ambitiously developed the island between 1964 and 1976, dramatically reshaping it through a dredge-and-fill process that created miles of waterfront property. Ultimately halted by regulations stemming from a growing environmental movement in the United States, the Mackles' impact on Marco Island was lasting, transformational, and irreversible.

In the years since, Marco Island has learned to stand on its own two feet, electing to incorporate as a city on August 28, 1997. With that decision came jurisdiction over its own roads, bridge, storm drainage, utilities, and parks. Cultural attractions have sprung up on the island, thanks largely to private fundraising efforts, including the Marco Island Center for the Arts in 2002 and the Marco Island Historical Museum in 2010. Businesses such as the Hilton and J.W. Marriott hotels, important contributors to Marco Island's economy, have undergone major renovations. The island was even touted as TripAdvisor's No. 1 island in the United States and No. 4 in the world in 2014.

Today, the city of Marco Island is a popular international tourist destination home to more than 16,000 residents. During the season, which is typically at its peak between December and March, the island's population swells to over 40,000 people. Most of Marco Island's year-round economy is sustained by these crucial months. As more new people continue to visit Marco Island, the Marco Island Historical Society will continue to educate and inspire an appreciation for its storied history. At the Marco Island Historical Museum, the island's history is brought to life by award-winning exhibits and state-of-the-art collections preservation.

This book explores a period of dramatic transformation and intense development on Marco Island, from 1962 to present. From the Mackles' original vision for the island to Hurricane Irma, this pictorial history outlines the events and milestones in between, each contributing in some way to what it means today to be a Marco Islander.

One

AN ISLAND
UNTO THEMSELVES

Seen here from left to right, developers Robert (1911–1983), Frank (1916–1993), and Elliott Mackle (1908–1878), also known as "Florida's Famous Mackle Brothers," founded the Deltona Corporation in 1962. Together, they formulated an ambitious plan to transform Marco Island from an idyllic tropical island with a population of only a few hundred to a full-scale residential community home to more than 35,000 people. Their vision shaped the Marco Island of today.

$500 Million Development Planned For Marco Island

F. E. MACKLE, Jr.
President,
Deltona Corporation

-- The Deltona Corporation today launched a venture jointly with a group of prominent investors for the development of Marco Island on Collier County's Gulf Coast -- with long-term expenditures scheduled to top a half-billion dollars.

The Miami-based construction and development corporation announced that it has teamed up with an investor group in which major interests are held by Peter N. Thomson, Canadian investment and industrial executive; Gerry Brothers & Co., a New York private investment firm; Barron Collier Jr., son of the late advertising executive and pioneer Florida developer, and Mrs. Isabel Collier Read, sister-in law of Collier.

Together, they established Marco Island Development Corporation, whose initial funds will be $4.5 million and which is owned 50 percent by The Deltona Corporation and 50 per cent by the investor group.

Frank E. Mackle Jr. president of The Deltona Corporation, said that the jointly owned firm will develop a total of approximately 10,100 acres on Marco Island, adjoining smaller islands and nearby mainland. The property juts into the Gulf of Mexico some 12 miles south of Naples.

LAST FRONTIER

"Marco Island is the last large undeveloped tract of waterfront land in South Florida," said Mackle, "and its rolling topography and tropical foliage give it a character unmatched in this part of the world. We are determined that the community we build there will be fully in keeping with the island's natural beauty and ideal location."

IDYLLIC MARCO ISLAND, 26 miles southeast of Naples, with its seemingly endless beach rimmed by Australian pines, gumbo-limbo trees and rare twisting vines, was purchased today by the Deltona Corporation, which is headed by Frank B. Mackle, Jr. The six-mile long isle, completely unspoiled and remote, yet not isolated, is the last undeveloped tract of waterfront land in South Florida. Air photo shows only the north extremity of the island with Big Marco Pass to the left and the tiny village of Marco at rear center. Today not a single house dots the wide sandy shore where rare shells are found in profusion. The Deltona Corporation plans to develop 10,100 acres on Marco and the adjoining islands. (McGrath photo)

'We'll Keep Beauty' - Mackle

The Mackles first visited Marco Island in 1962 after receiving a letter of interest from Barron Collier Jr., son of advertising and real estate magnate Barron G. Collier. The Colliers had owned most of Marco Island since 1922, but plans for its development stalled since the elder Collier's passing in 1939. In March 1964, the Colliers and the Mackles reached a deal with the establishment of the Marco Island Development Corporation (MIDC). The MIDC was split evenly between the Deltona Corporation and an investment group including the Colliers. The group set a price tag of $7 million, centering the deal for Marco Island around a 10-year repayment plan. Deltona could withhold its first payment interest-free until 1968 before initiating six years of payments for full rights to the island. The long-term project would cost Deltona an estimated $500 million.

10

The Mackles envisioned Marco Island as a full-scale self-sufficient island community. According to Frank Mackle Jr., more than 10,000 acres planned for development would be "fully in keeping with the island's natural beauty." The ambitious plan included "facilities for every conceivable community need and for every kind of Florida living," with affordable housing for middle-class families and designated areas for schools, churches, recreation, public utilities, and commercial buildings. The photograph above shows Marco Island in 1964, just prior to its development. The scale model below shows Marco Island as the Mackles first envisioned it. James Vensel, Deltona's vice president of architecture, was entrusted with creating the Mackles' comprehensive master plan, mapping out more than 12,000 homesites, 125 miles of paved roads, and 90 miles of navigable waterways—all over Memorial Day weekend in 1964.

THIS SCALE MODEL SHOWS A
REVEALING LOOK INTO THE FUTURE

In 1964, Marco Island's remote location and relative lack of infrastructure presented major challenges to its developers. There was no dependable source of drinking water, no sewage system, and no cultural or recreational facilities on the island. Mosquitoes were a major nuisance, and much of Marco's buildable land was still underwater. Vensel's master plan called for a complete physical transformation of Marco Island. Construction began in June 1964, soon after the Mackles finalized a deal with the Colliers. With a target grand opening set for January 1965, Deltona had less than eight months to build the facilities and infrastructure necessary to host large numbers of prospective buyers. The left photograph shows heavy machinery smoothing out roads on Marco Island on May 7, 1965. The photograph below shows construction workers driving cement pilings for a bridge on April 24, 1965.

Vensel plotted most of the homes on Marco Island along "finger" canals that only existed on paper, requiring Deltona to both dig the canals and create hundreds of acres of new waterfront property. Earth was dredged from swampland, as well as from nearby bays, to raise the elevation of homesites to a required three feet above high tide. A barge held the dredge in place as powerful pumps sucked up earth and propelled it through a series of pipes to the fill site. This "dredge and fill" process simultaneously created new land for houses and deeper waterways for boats. The photograph above shows the dredge working around what would become Bimini Avenue and Butterfield Court on May 20, 1965. The photograph below shows 12 model homes plotted along Chestnut Court finger canals on February 27, 1965.

To make Marco Island's new land suitable for building, future homesites were reinforced with concrete pilings and seawalls to prevent erosion. Deltona's constant need for concrete led to the formation of its own mixing plant at the site of the former Air Force missile tracking station on the south end of Marco Island's beach, today Cape Marco. Between 1965 and 1968, the plant produced an estimated 120,000 tons of concrete, saving the MIDC an estimated 20 percent over the cost of ready-mixed concrete. The photograph above shows three cement mixing trucks at the facility, each with a door emblazoned with the MIDC's distinctive "M" logo. The photograph below shows Ed White, electronics technician, mixing a truckload of concrete via the control panel. Both photographs were captured on October 4, 1970, by Bryan Donaldson.

THE MARCO ISLAND YACHT CLUB

(Club completed January 1965)

In addition to developing Marco Island's infrastructure prior to opening day, the Mackles focused construction on what they envisioned would be the primary attractions to visitors. These included the 50-room Marco Beach Hotel, the sales/administration office, 22 model homes, and the Marco Island Yacht Club. Remarkably, all were completed in time for the January 31, 1965, opening. The total cost of construction and development between June 1964 and January 1965 exceeded $4 million. The image above shows an artist's rendering of the Marco Island Yacht Club, which was completed in January 1965. The image below shows an artist's rendering of the sales/administration office.

ADMINISTRATION BUILDING

Marco Island's grand opening on January 31, 1965, was successful thanks to an effective marketing campaign by Neil Bahr, Deltona's chief sales executive and head of marketing. Approximately 25,000 people came to Marco Island by air, land, and sea to catch a glimpse of the Mackles' alluring new project. Deltona sales agents were stationed throughout the island to greet the larger than expected crowds. For those who drove to the island, the first stop was likely the sales/administration office (above). The office served as an orientation point for unfamiliar visitors and was located at the present site of the Marco Island Fire Department, at what is now the intersection of Bald Eagle Drive and San Marco Road. The photograph below, taken on January 31, 1965, shows a busy parking lot in front of the sales/administration office. (Above, photograph by John Maerker.)

Visitors had several options for exploration from the sales/administration office. The beach was an obvious destination for many, including those staying at the new 50-room Marco Beach Hotel. An observation tower at the south end of Marco Island offered panoramic views of the spectacular scenery, and food and drinks were served at the brand-new Marco Island Yacht Club. The main attractions, however, were the 22 model homes lining Chestnut Court and Tahiti Road. Each had a unique design, offering prospective buyers a variety of possibilities. The 12 waterfront Chestnut homes were priced as low as $19,800, and the 10 inland Tahiti homes started at $14,900. The right photograph shows the Marco Beach Hotel under expansion from 50 to 100 rooms in November 1965. The self-guided tour map below, printed about 1967, shows what was available to visitors at the time.

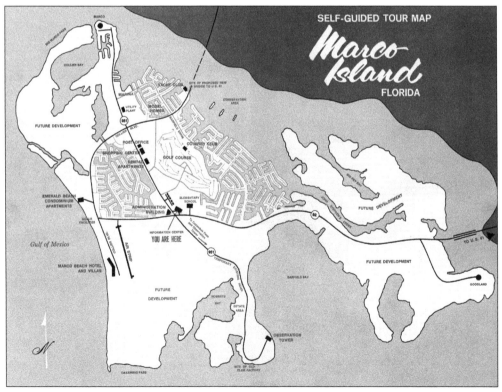

SELF-GUIDED TOUR MAP

Marco Island

FLORIDA

By 1970, Deltona had netted more than $100 million in home and homesite sales, and the population surpassed 2,700, after beginning at less than 600 in 1964. Marco Island was so successful that the original 1964 agreement with the Collier group was resolved immediately in 1968, granting Deltona full control over the development rights to Marco Island. The left photograph, taken in 1970, shows construction work beginning on the new Marco Beach Hotel, just south of and adjacent to the original Marco Beach Hotel & Villas. The photograph below looks north and shows the intersection of Bald Eagle Drive and San Marco Road on October 8, 1981. The large vacant lot in the center is now the Marco Island Urgent Care Center. The Deltona sales/administration office is visible to the right. (Below, photograph by Smith Aerial Photography, Inc.)

Neil Bahr's "Coordinated Growth Plan" drove Deltona's early success on Marco Island. Marco was divided into five areas (Marco River, Roberts Bay, Collier Bay, Barfield Bay/Blue Hill, and Big Key) to be developed individually over time to accommodate the three-year time frame attached to each federal dredge-and-fill permit. Bahr's plan enabled buyers who could not afford full payment up front to submit monthly installments (plus five-percent interest) on future developments. Finance plans for the initial development in the Marco River area were available for up to three years, and properties in the Barfield Bay and Big Key areas could be financed for up to 10 years. The c. 1970 image above shows the master plan for Marco Island, with different planned phases of development. The photograph below shows Marco Island in October 1969 with construction visible in the Roberts Bay (left) and Marco River (right) areas.

The US Army Corps of Engineers required any permitted dredge-and-fill work to be completed within three years. For Deltona, which required county, state, and federal permits for all five planned phases of its operation at Marco Island, the first permit in 1964 (Marco River area) was approved in four months. Deltona applied for its second permit (Roberts Bay area) in 1967, but the Department of the Interior recommended its denial in September 1968 in response to growing pressure from environmental groups. The permit was eventually issued in December 1969, but with a warning that future applications may not be "similarly granted." The photograph above shows the recently developed Marco River (north of Barfield Bay) area in June 1973. The photograph below shows the Marco River area looking north in December 1972. (Above, courtesy of the National Archives and Records Administration.)

By the late 1960s, an environmental movement was gaining momentum in the United States. The passage of the National Environmental Policy Act of 1969 and the Clean Water Act of 1972, as well as the formation of the Environmental Protection Agency in 1970, meant increasingly complex hurdles in the permitting process for Deltona. After a lengthy struggle over the Roberts Bay permit, Deltona became concerned with Marco's three remaining permit areas. The company attempted to proactively address environmental concerns, establishing the Marco Applied Marine Ecology Station (MAMES) in 1971 to conduct scientific studies on marine resources in the Marco area. The photograph above shows the MAMES in April 1973. The photograph below shows University of West Florida marine biology student Bill Sirmans at the MAMES, studying oysters collected from the waters around Marco Island. (Above, photograph by John Maerker.)

In 1973, Deltona applied for permits to develop the remaining Barfield Bay/Blue Hill, Big Key, and Collier Bay areas. Although 90 percent of the Barfield Bay/Blue Hill and Big Key areas had already been sold, Deltona halted further land sales in anticipation of possible delays. Many customers refused to make further payments, and Deltona posted losses of more than $5 million in 1974 and 1975. Some locals and laborers supported Deltona, but environmentalists cited reports that argued for the importance of estuarine mangroves. In April 1976, the Corps denied the Barfield Bay/Blue Hill and Big Key areas, approving only the Collier Bay area for development. The left photograph shows a mangrove replanting study undertaken by Deltona and the MAMES in 1972. The image below shows an April 16, 1976, headline in the *Marco Eagle*. (Below, courtesy of the *Marco Eagle*.)

MARCO ISLAND

1776 ★★ 1976

THURSDAY, APRIL 22, 1976   MARCO ISLAND, FLORIDA   15 CENTS

Permits: 2 No's And 1 Yes

In a controversial and far-reaching decision the Federal government has turned down two of the three dredge and fill permit applications sought by The Deltona Corp. to complete development of Marco Island.

The U.S. Army Corps of Engineers announced last Friday in Washington that it has denied Deltona permits to develop 4,307 homesites on Big Key and in the Barfield Bay-Blue Hill Bay areas of this waterfront resort community.

The Corps granted Deltona's application for a permit to resume development of 1,400 homesites and commercial units in the Collier Bay area. About 40 homes and 36 percent of development in this area was halted by the Corps in 1971.

Deltona fought back with lawsuits but still held roughly 4,000 undeliverable homesites, towards which customers had already paid more than $77 million. Rather than declare bankruptcy, the Mackles offered several options, the last of which was a full refund—plus interest—paid over three years. To keep the company afloat, Deltona pursued the rapid development of condominiums such as the South Seas Club and Summit House in the late 1970s and early 1980s. In 1981, the courts ruled against Deltona, and a settlement turned most of its undeveloped lands into nature preserves. The Mackles resigned from the Deltona Corporation in 1986. The photograph above shows the construction of the Sandcastle and Charter Club condominiums on December 16, 1981. The c. 1980 photograph below shows the South Seas Towers and Sunset House North condominiums. (Above, photograph by Smith Aerial Photography, Inc.)

For more than 20 years, the Mackles fought for their ambitious vision of a planned island community. Though ultimately forced to withdraw, many of their dreams were realized, leaving an immeasurable impact on today's Marco Island. A unique balance of civilization and nature was born out of compromise, rooted in the courtroom decisions of the 1970s and 1980s. Today, Marco Island is one of the most popular island destinations in the world thanks largely to its special blend of culture and wildlife. The photograph above shows Marco Island on March 11, 1991, five years after the Mackles formally removed themselves from its development. The photograph below shows a view from above Marco Island looking northeast in 2017. (Above, photograph by Smith Aerial Photography, Inc.; below, photograph by Joey Waves.)

Two

SELLING SWAMPLAND
IN FLORIDA

The Mackles' dream for Marco Island might have remained just that if not for their enormous investments in a national marketing campaign. There simply were not enough local buyers to fulfill their projections of a 6,000-percent increase in population, especially given Marco Island's relatively remote location. This image shows the cover of a 12-page advertising supplement published on opening day, January 31, 1965, in the *Orlando Sentinel* and other major newspapers.

Neil Bahr (1925–2010) was Deltona's chief sales executive and head of marketing. Marco Island presented a unique challenge for Bahr, as he was tasked with selling thousands of undeveloped lots using only the Mackles' glittering reputation and the promise that Marco Island would become a desirable place to live. After the Mackles received the green light to develop the island in June 1964, Bahr hit the ground running. The MIDC's entire capital would be spent by the grand opening in January 1965, making immediate sales essential to the project's continuation. The photograph below shows Neil Bahr (center) with Frank (left) and Robert Mackle (right). (Left, courtesy of the *Marco Eagle*; below, courtesy of the Bahr family archives.)

Bahr expanded Deltona's network of franchised agents by more than 70 percent in 1964. More than half of all homes—and nearly three out of every four lots—were presold by agents outside of Florida. This photograph shows Deltona salesman Richard "Dick" Teibel accepting an award for superior performance at the 1969 convention of Deltona Corporation dealerships. Also pictured are Neil Bahr (left), Elliott Mackle, and Bernard Vespucci (director of sales, right).

Herbert R. Savage (born 1919), Deltona's chief architect, was most responsible for the early theme of Marco Island. Savage was inspired by Hawaii, incorporating a Polynesian style into the design of numerous buildings. Prior to opening day, Savage designed the administration/sales office, Marco Beach Hotel, Marco Island Yacht Club, and 22 model homes. The same style is prevalent throughout Deltona's marketing materials. In this photograph, Savage (right) is showing a group of people a wall display of model homes in Deltona, another Mackle-built community.

In October 2016, after operating out of the same office on Collier Boulevard since 1979, Savage retired at the age of 97. A World War II veteran, Savage has embraced his role as a historical icon of Marco Island and is a regular presence at community events. In recent years, he has had an alleyway and a bridge on Marco Island named in his honor, as well as an exhibit hall at the Marco Island Historical Museum, where he donated numerous records and photographs to the Marco Island Historical Society. The photograph above shows Savage (right) cutting cake with Frank Mackle Jr. and Frank Mackle III. The left photograph shows Savage standing in front of a tower that he designed at what is now the J.W. Marriott (formerly the Marco Beach Hotel) in 2000.

As opening day drew closer, Bahr rolled out a massive $600,000 media blitz. The campaign proved wildly effective, resulting in more than 50,000 letters of inquiry in the first month alone. Approximately 25,000 people visited Marco Island on January 31, 1965—to see firsthand what the Mackles had been building—thanks largely to Bahr's effective marketing campaign. A three-dimensional scale model of "completed" Marco Island was on display in the sales/administration office, and Bahr was there in person to field questions. The c. 1969 photograph above shows a crowd gathered around a scale model in the sales/administration office. The photograph below shows what is likely the same model. An original Deltona model is now preserved and frequently displayed at the Marco Island Historical Museum in its Modern Marco Island exhibit.

Get all
the facts
on a new
Tropic Island
Future
in Florida!

First Class
Permit No. 1
Marco Island, Fla.

BUSINESS REPLY MAIL
No postage stamp necessary if mailed in the United States

POSTAGE WILL BE PAID BY

MACKLE BROS. DIVISION
MARCO ISLAND DEVELOPMENT
THE DELTONA CORPORATION
MARCO ISLAND, FLORIDA 33937

The sheer ambition and scale of Bahr's advertising campaign was a factor in its success. On January 31, 1965, twelve-page color supplements (see page 25) advertising Marco Island ran in 30 major newspapers, including the *New York Times, Boston Herald,* and *Chicago Tribune.* Bus placards, billboards, and nearly 700 television and radio spots introduced Marco Island to the entire country. As an example of the campaign's pervasiveness, a television commercial for Marco Island can be overheard in a scene in the Academy Award–winning 1971 film *The French Connection.* The image above shows an example of the business reply mail cards that Deltona included in much of its marketing materials. The photograph below shows television personality Jack Paar (left) and Elliott Mackle (right) at the Marco Beach Hotel. In 1968, Paar hosted a promotional film titled *At Marco Island with Jack Paar.*

The Mackles' vision of an all-inclusive community was reflected in the diversity of their model homes. Between 1965 and 1975, Deltona unveiled 72 unique model homes on Marco Island, attracting buyers of many different tastes and income levels. Property values have skyrocketed since, while real estate remains a dominant local industry. The image above shows an artist's rendering of the Martinique model, first offered on Marco Island in 1965. Described as a "spacious waterway home with the simplicity of tropical elegance," the three-bedroom, two-bath home sold for $41,500, the most expensive home available in 1965. The photograph below shows one of Deltona's model homes after construction.

Nearly every building that Herbert Savage designed shared a common design feature: an unobstructed view of the water from inside the entryway. The Mackles had specifically requested this element, and it became a staple in Savage's later creations, such as the Marco Island Country Club and the expanded Marco Beach Hotel & Villas. It also appeared in the model homes that Savage designed, 22 of which were available in 1965. The left photograph shows Savage (left) talking about a model home on Marco Island with interior designers Bob Paulding (center) and Bill Goode (right) of Fort Lauderdale on April 9, 1970. The photograph below shows a group of prospective buyers touring Deltona's five new model homes designed by Savage along Collier Boulevard on July 4, 1973. (Left, photograph by Bryan Donaldson.)

Marco Island was featured in the January 1967 edition of *Reader's Digest*, a monthly magazine that had the largest circulation in the world at the time. A three-page full-color ad in the national magazine was seen by an estimated 17 million readers. This represented phase one of a two-phase promotional effort announced by the MIDC in 1966 to reach 50 million people. Its goal was to "through some of the world's best-known media, [offer] the opportunity to own property in one of the most unique pre-planned communities ever conceived." At right is a promotional image from the January 1967 issue of *Reader's Digest*. The image below shows the cover of a promotional packet produced by Deltona.

¡EXOTICA ISLA
EN LA FLORIDA!

Una Esmeralda bañada
por las cálidas aguas
del Golfo de México

Marco Island
CONSTRUIDA POR LOS MACKLE

The Mackles' original vision for Marco Island included housing for middle-class working families and people of all income levels, not just seasonal residents and retirees. Their company cast a broad net from the outset, with more than 100 authorized sales agencies and branch offices worldwide. They targeted marketing heavily in the Midwestern and Northeastern United States and established an international presence in Latin America, Western Europe, and Asia. The left image shows a Spanish promotional brochure for Marco Island, "*construida por los Mackle.*" The image below shows a 1970 advertisement for Marco Island emphasizing an upcoming price increase.

THEY HAVE IT MADE...

AT MARCO ISLAND, FLORIDA ...
WILL YOU?
PRICES INCREASE 15% MARCH 31, 1970

The *Marco Islander* was a popular sightseeing boat constructed for Deltona in 1968. Another effective marketing tool, the 40-foot-long, 20-foot-wide vessel offered up to 32 prospective buyers free rides and a unique view of Marco Island from the water. The Polynesian-style boat tied in with Deltona's predominant South Seas theme for Marco Island. The thatched palmetto roof, modeled after a Seminole chickee, provided a local connection. The vessel cost an estimated $60,000 to build and was constructed in West Palm Beach, Florida. Powered by twin diesel engines, the completed catamaran debuted on Labor Day 1968 at the opening ceremony for the Marco River toll bridge (now the S.S. Jolley Bridge). The c. 1970 postcard above shows the *Marco Islander* on the water. The right photograph shows Miami artist Anthony Lopez carving the signature four-foot tiki heads from fiberglass.

In 1972, under the guidance of chief pilot Ray Anderson, the Deltona Corporation founded Marco Island Airways (MIA). The fleet started with three 15-passenger Beechcraft B-99 aircraft but quickly expanded to include six 40-passenger Martin 4-0-4 airliners. Marco Island Airways flew five round-trip flights per day between Miami and Marco Island, requiring its own ticket counter at Miami International Airport. In the early 1980s, direct flights were added to Tampa and Lakeland, further connecting Marco Island to airports around the world. After several years of declining passenger numbers, the airline was bought out by Provincetown-Boston Airlines in 1984. The photograph above shows one of MIA's Martin 4-0-4 airliners. The 1977 photograph below shows MIA flight attendant Dawn Dahnke Norgren serving in-flight beverages. (Above, courtesy of David Henderson.)

When Marco Island opened in 1965, there was a small airstrip just two blocks from the Marco Beach Hotel, near what is now Landmark Street. Arriving guests boarded a shuttle and had a clear view of the beach from the hotel lobby within minutes. The airstrip was relocated in 1968, when Marco Island Airways upgraded to a 4,000-foot runway and four-building terminal near what is now Edgewater Court. The airport was relocated again in 1976 to Marco Shores (at the east end of Mainsail Drive), eventually becoming what is now the Marco Island Executive Airport. The photograph above shows the 3,100-foot-long airstrip on Marco Island, which was widened in 1965 to accommodate larger planes and increased traffic. The photograph below shows the airport terminal on Marco Island in 1970.

the Marco Islander

WINTER 1967

The Deltona Corporation produced the *Marco Islander* magazine from 1965 to 1979. What started as a small monthly newsletter gradually expanded into a colorful quarterly publication that was distributed freely to Marco Island property owners and anyone else interested in "hearing the Marco Island story." The magazine charted the growth and development of Marco Island through articles about construction projects, business openings, community events, and more. Originally designed to attract prospective buyers to Marco Island, the publication now serves as a valuable educational resource, capturing an authentic slice of life during a period of rapid development. The winter 1967 cover of the *Marco Islander* above shows two women on a tandem bicycle in front of the Marco Beach Hotel & Villas. The MIHS has a complete collection of the magazine, which has been digitized and placed on exhibit at the Marco Island Historical Museum.

Three

MARCO'S MAGNETISM

To a salesperson, there are probably few locations in the United States more ideally situated than Marco Island. The subtropical island practically sells itself with its dramatic sunset views, white sand beach, and verdant landscape teeming with wildlife. Yet there is more to Marco Island than its natural splendor. Clever marketers have also been crafting and selling an idea of Marco Island, beginning with Neil Bahr's campaign in the 1960s.

The Marco sari was a popular all-purpose women's garment in the late 1960s and early 1970s. It debuted on July 19, 1968, at a private fashion show in the lounge of the Emerald Beach Condominium. Creator Norene Barnes was inspired by a friend's rave reviews of the comfortable Hawaiian muumuu. Motivated by her love for Marco Island, Barnes created an entire line of saris that embodied Marco's casual island lifestyle. The versatile dress could be worn anywhere—from the beach to a formal dinner party—and came in a variety of colors and exotic fabrics. The left photograph shows Barnes (right) and Wendy Wine modeling saris. The photograph below shows 12 women, including Barnes and Wine (left), modeling saris at the Emerald Beach on July 19, 1968.

Beginning in the 1960s, Marco Island was subtly sold by its promoters as a place to see and be seen. Many of the models pictured in Deltona's marketing campaign were young, attractive, and stylish. Although perhaps not truly representative of the island's resident population, the imagery created a sense of decorum and appropriate fashion for many visitors. The right photograph shows Barbara Hornsby posing with a scooter in front of the Marco Beach Hotel & Villas. Her colorful ensemble is one of four described in the summer/fall 1967 issue of the *Marco Islander* magazine, each featuring "vibrant colors capturing the lure of the 'South Seas,' the latest in resort fashions at semi-tropical Marco Island." The photograph below shows a fashionable couple dining at the Marco Beach Hotel & Villas.

Tony Lema (1934–1966) was a professional golfer who was named the first touring pro at the Marco Island Country Club in 1965. Dubbed "Champagne Tony," Lema won the 1964 Open Championship at just 30 years old. Lema's life and promising career were cut short on July 24, 1966, when he and his wife, Betty, were killed in a plane crash. The Mackles created an annual pro-am golf tournament, the Tony Lema Memorial, in his honor. The first tournament was held on February 28, 1967, at the Marco Island Country Club and drew more than 3,000 people. The first foursome included, from left to right (below), Frank Mackle Jr., Gene Sarazen, Richard Nixon, and Gordon Biggars. The photograph above shows Richard Nixon hitting the opening ball of the 1967 tournament, which went "straight as a string for 225 yards," as reported in the Spring-Summer 1967 *Marco Islander*. (Above, photograph by Howard Holsberg.)

The trend of high-profile celebrity participation in the Tony Lema Memorial continued for 13 years until the last tournament in 1980. Another effective marketing tool for Deltona, the challenging 6,800-yard golf course appealed to professional golfers like Jack Nicklaus, Arnold Palmer, and Lee Trevino, while the glamour of the club drew celebrities such as baseball icon Joe DiMaggio, actor James Garner, and Miami Dolphins football coach Don Shula. The celebrities, in turn, attracted thousands of onlookers each year, many seeking autographs or photographs. The right photograph shows Nicklaus (left) and comedian Bob Hope (right) at a charity event on Marco Island in March 1973. The photograph below shows the award ceremony for the 1971 Tony Lema Memorial, won by Bobby Nichols with a score of 66, at the Marco Island Country Club.

Nicklaus and Hope during their exhibition round

A.

Gene Sarazen (1902–1999) is one of golf's all-time greats, winning seven major tournaments and a career grand slam between 1922 and 1935. Sarazen's most memorable golf moment came at the 1935 Masters Tournament, where he hit the "shot heard 'round the world"—a double eagle on the final-round 15th hole to make up a three-shot deficit. Sarazen came to Marco Island in 1966 and was an active leader and philanthropist in the community for more than 30 years. He was named permanent chairman of the Marco Island Country Club's Golf Committee in 1967 and served as its resident professional from 1981 to 1999. The left photograph shows Sarazen standing next to a bust of Tony Lema at the first Tony Lema Memorial in 1967. The photograph below shows Sarazen with friend Ken Venturi (1931–2013), another golf legend and a popular television commentator who lived on Marco Island from 1976 to 2002.

Dalia "Dale" Messick (1906–2005) was an American cartoonist who created the popular comic strip series *Brenda Starr, Reporter*. At its peak popularity in the 1950s, the comic strip appeared in 250 newspapers. Messick was a winter resident of Marco Island, buying a house in 1965 after visiting the island for inspiration to draw a treasure-hunting episode. Messick reportedly bought the house "because it looked a little like an artist's studio." On December 18, 1966, Messick dedicated a statue of her character Margo the Marco Island Mermaid outside of the Marco Beach Hotel (right). The statue is still on display at what is now the J.W. Marriott, just north of Quinn's Restaurant on the beach. The photograph below shows Messick working on cartoons at her Marco Island home.

You can drive to this island

Historically, Marco Island was not an easy place to get to. The first road to the island was completed by about 1912 but ended at a ferry crossing on the other side of the Marco River, at what is now Isles of Capri. The first bridge to the island, a wooden swing bridge, was put in place near Goodland in 1938. The Mackles recognized the challenges presented by the island's remoteness, meeting them head-on by building an airport in 1965 and two new concrete bridges in 1969 and 1975. The island's accessibility was heavily promoted to quell any fears buyers might have about purchasing a home on Marco Island. The left image shows an advertisement for the Goodland Bridge in 1976. The c. 1970 image below shows an advertisement encouraging people to fly their own planes to Marco Island.

fly your own plane to **Marco Island** *Florida*

Fishing has been one of Marco Island's primary attractions for thousands of years. The Calusa Indians and their ancestors lived on Marco Island for more than 6,000 years, thriving on a diet consisting primarily of fish and shellfish. Fishing was also an important industry during Marco Island's pioneer era, especially as tourists began flocking to the area during the tarpon craze of the late 1800s. Sport fishing has been a staple ever since, and Marco Island is world-renowned for its plentiful waters. Popular local game fish include tarpon, snook, shark, and red drum (also known as redfish). Recreational fishing was promoted heavily by the Deltona Corporation as one of Marco Island's primary attractants, promising "superb fishing from boat, pier, or beach." Naturally, there were no guarantees—but the promotional photographs never showed an empty line.

FISHING AT *Marco Island*

DETAILED INFORMATION ON HOW AND WHERE TO CATCH THEM, BY RUSS SMILEY

Boating excitement at

Marco Island

Just as fishing has occurred on Marco Island for several millennia, so too has boating. For the Calusa and their ancestors, boating was more than a recreational activity—it was a way of life. "Pioneer" Marco Islanders also relied on boats for transportation until the first vehicular bridge to the island was built in 1938. As Marco Island transitioned into its modern era under the direction of the Mackle brothers, boats became objects of luxury rather than necessity. Understanding the allure of Marco's surrounding waters, the Mackles purposefully developed the island with roughly 75 percent of all homes situated along waterfront property and encouraged home buyers to make room for a personal watercraft. Today, boating is one of the most popular recreational activities at Marco Island. The photograph below shows the *Marco Islander* catamaran, which provided free tours to prospective home buyers.

The Mackles regularly hosted large events to draw crowds and excitement to Marco Island. One such example was the Summerset Regatta, an annual sailboat race kicked off on Labor Day 1966 at the Marco Island Yacht Club. The event drew more than 500 people, leading Elliott Mackle to declare that "it seems we have a new annual tradition on our hands." His statement proved prophetic, as the Summerset Regatta completed its 53rd annual run in October 2018.

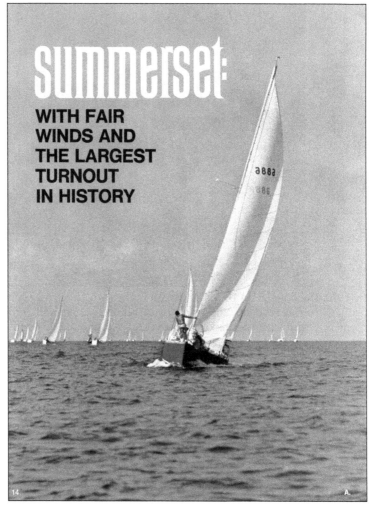

summerset:

WITH FAIR WINDS AND THE LARGEST TURNOUT IN HISTORY

Another popular annual event on Marco Island began in 1971 with the Antique Auto Show. Held on July 4, 1971, at the Marco Island Yacht Club, the first auto show attracted more than 30 antique cars from around the state of Florida, in turn attracting hundreds of interested onlookers. The Kiwanis Club of Marco Island now puts on its own annual car show each February.

By 1970, the population of Marco Island had grown to over 2,700, including more than 800 families. As new residents flocked to the island, local community groups sprang up, including a Woman's Club, Civic Association, Kiwanis Club, Rotary Club, Garden Club, and Flying Club. The new community groups, promoted extensively in Deltona's *Marco Islander* magazine and regular subjects of articles in the *Marco Eagle* newspaper, created a sense of identity and place for the many new families who were not native to the area. They also helped the Mackles sell the idea of Marco Island as a hospitable and friendly place to live. The photograph above shows members of the Marco Island Flying Club at the airport in 1971. The photograph below shows children and counselors building sand castles on the beach at the Marco Beach Hotel in 1972.

The opportunity for fun in the sun is one of Marco Island's most obvious attributes, and astute marketers have been capitalizing on related imagery for more than 50 years. A plethora of outdoor sporting activities is available through various businesses and community groups. Popular outdoor activities on Marco Island include golf, biking, paddle boarding, tennis, shuffleboard, softball, swimming, beach volleyball, and more recently, beach yoga and pickleball. Marco Island has hosted several major sporting events, most notably for golf and tennis. The right postcard shows tennis courts in use at the Marco Beach Hotel. The photograph below shows two women playing their own version of beach volleyball in front of the Emerald Beach Condominium in 1966.

The single most alluring feature of Marco Island, around which much of the local economy is now based, is its beach. The six-mile-long, crescent-shaped stretch of white sand along the Gulf of Mexico is one of the most beautiful publicly accessible beaches in Florida. It became the centerpiece around which Deltona's entire community plan would be based. More than half a century later, after intense development, several beach nourishment projects, and countless visitors, the same combination of sand, sun, and surf attracts people to Marco Island from around the world. The photograph above is from a 1967 brochure for the Marco Beach Hotel & Villas. The postcard below shows beachcombers scouring for shells with the Emerald Beach the only building visible in the background.

With so many fabricated opportunities for action and adventure on and around Marco Island, the quiet and natural moments are still sometimes the most memorable. Marco Island is famous for its sunsets, where beachgoers look for the green flash and often applaud the sun as it sinks below the horizon. Dolphin, bald eagle, and burrowing owl sightings spark excitement and wonder in people of all ages. In 1982, Marco Island was promoted as a place to "get away from it all . . . and have it all." Despite Marco Island's increasingly dense population, there still seems to be no shortage of opportunities to do both. The photograph above shows a couple on the beach at Marco Island in 1967. The photograph below shows John Maerker fishing the Marco River from underneath a sabal palm on Magnolia Court in June 1979.

The shoreline of Marco Island is constantly changing, as evidenced by Hurricane Irma in September 2017, which swept tons of sand and debris from Hideaway Beach into Collier Creek, blocking the popular boating route for months. As the effects of climate change cause global sea levels to continue to rise and intense storm activity to increase, Marco Island's treasured beach will doubtless be the subject of continued discussion, study, and hopefully, preventative action to mitigate potentially damaging effects to Marco Island's economy and environment. The photograph above shows Marco Island's beach in 1970. The photograph below looking south shows Tigertail Beach in 2002 or 2003. (Below, photograph by Don & Roy Couture.)

Four

ISLAND ICONS

Marco Island's identity lies as much in its iconic buildings and places as it does in its natural grandeur. These landmarks were—and in some cases, still are—the settings for countless memories made by residents and visitors alike during the past half-century. The Emerald Beach Condominium (pictured) was Marco Island's first high-rise, shown here in 1966.

Construction on the $800,000 fifty-room Marco Beach Hotel began in June 1964, less than eight months before it opened in January 1965. It featured a large pool and a nine-hole "pitch and putt" golf course with an unobstructed view of the Gulf of Mexico. Demand for the hotel was so great that the MIDC expanded it to 100 rooms in November 1965, also adding 12 new luxury Polynesian Villas (six buildings, two villas each), a shuffleboard court, and a tennis court. By 1967, the Marco Beach Hotel & Villas boasted 22 villas, a convention hall, the Voyager Room restaurant, and the Sand Bar Lounge. Single-occupancy rooms cost $20 per night, and two-bedroom villas cost as much as $95 per night. The photograph above shows the Marco Beach Hotel & Villas around 1966. The postcard below was printed sometime after 1967.

While the original Marco Beach Hotel & Villas (pictured above) proved successful, the Mackles still envisioned a world-class beach resort on Marco Island. Plans for a new 370-room hotel began in 1968. The $17.5-million project included a 10-story hotel room tower, 15 meeting rooms, a 100-booth exhibition hall, a pool, tennis courts, and several dining options. The new hotel reported advance bookings of approximately $5 million and employed a staff of over 400. The expansion opened on December 18, 1971, just south of the original hotel (which became the Voyager section). The hotel was a crowning achievement for the Mackles and was purchased by Marriott in 1979. The photograph below shows, from left to right, Archbishop Coleman Carroll, Robert Mackle, Florida governor Reubin Askew, Frank Mackle Jr., Neil Bahr, and Roger Everingham at the dedication ceremony in December 1971.

At Frank Mackle Jr.'s request, architect Herbert Savage was commissioned to design the new Marco Beach Hotel & Villas. In 1968, Mackle sent Savage to Hawaii, where he found inspiration for a grandiose Polynesian-style resort. The spectacular lobby became the hotel's signature element. A raised porte cochère on Collier Boulevard and a 100-foot window expanse overlooking the Gulf of Mexico gave guests an immediate view of the pool and beach. The postcard above shows the iconic entrance and adjacent tower, built in 1971. The left photograph shows the hotel lobby in 1972. On January 1, 2017, the hotel officially became the J.W. Marriott Marco Island Beach Resort, undergoing yet another major expansion. Savage's signature entrance, although reimagined stylistically in recent years, remains largely as he first envisioned it.

Marco Island has been home to three different airports since 1965. The first airstrip, operational with a 3,100-foot runway by 1965, was located on what is now Landmark Street, just two blocks from the Marco Beach Hotel. Passengers were conveniently whisked from the airstrip to the hotel within minutes of arrival. Due to planned dredging near the first airstrip, a new 4,000-foot airstrip was constructed in October 1968 (pictured at right) near what is now Edgewater Court. Deltona, however, always intended for the airport to be on the mainland. In September 1976, to better serve its estimated 50,000 passengers per year from Miami, Deltona built the Marco Island Airport at the end of what is now Mainsail Drive. The photograph below shows the grand opening of what is now the Marco Island Executive Airport in 1976.

Churches were always part of the Mackles' master plan for Marco Island. Several tracts were gifted to qualified congregations planning a house of worship. St. Mark's Episcopal Church was the first modern church constructed on Marco Island. More than 100 worshippers gathered for the opening service on January 22, 1967, in the new $58,000 building. The photograph above shows the church in May 1968. (Photograph by John Maerker.)

The second church on the island was the United Church of Marco Island. The $146,000 structure was built on five acres of land donated by the Deltona Corporation on North Barfield Drive and Barbados Avenue. Members attended the first service in the Tahitian-style structure with 10 stained-glass windows in March 1972.

The construction of Marco Island's first condominium, Emerald Beach, was another important milestone in Deltona's master plan. The seven-story beachfront building opened in March 1966. Designed by Deltona architect Herbert Savage, the condominium features 48 one- and two-bedroom apartments. The $1.5-million structure was "designed to meet the varied needs for luxury living on the island." The entire condominium sold out within the first year, with prices ranging from $19,900 to $49,500 per apartment. Emerald Beach is still a sought-after condominium and continues to serve as a reminder of Marco Island's history. The architectural rendering above shows a scale model of the Emerald Beach prior to construction. The photograph below shows the completed building in 1966.

The MIDC unveiled the Marco Island Country Club on February 5, 1966, just over one year after Marco Island's grand opening. An estimated 300 spectators attended the dedication ceremony. The inaugural first round was played by "Champagne Tony" Lema, US senator George A. Smathers, Gene Sarazen, and Frank Mackle Jr. The 18-hole, par-72 course was designed by Dave Wallace and cost $500,000 to build. After just five years of successful operation, the club underwent a $1.5-million expansion. The new club debuted on March 5, 1971, showcasing a swimming pool and tennis courts in addition to building enhancements. The photograph above shows the club around 1966. (Emerald Beach is visible in the background.) The image below is a scorecard from the mid-1970s.

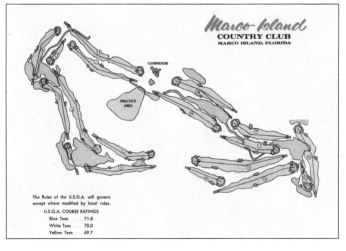

The MIDC spent $150,000 of its initial $500,000 budget on the Marco Island Country Club's clubhouse. In keeping with the Polynesian theme already established throughout the island, the clubhouse was a perfect complement to the championship golf course. Designed by James Vensel and Herbert Savage, the exteriors featured Florida keystone (limestone), pastel-colored stucco, natural stained wood, and peaked cedar shake roofs. The original buildings contained locker rooms, card rooms, offices, space for golf carts, a pro shop, and the 19th Hole lounge. The 1971 expansion added 29,500 square feet to the clubhouse, including five new buildings. The architectural rendering above shows plans for the clubhouse in October 1965. The photograph below shows guests enjoying the 19th Hole.

The 1,595-foot-long, 55-foot-high Marco River Bridge opened to great fanfare on December 13, 1969. The bridge cost $2.1 million to build, and the project took 15 months from beginning to end. Robert Mackle noted that "the bridge will cut 12 miles off the driving distance from Naples, thereby encouraging untold thousands of additional persons to visit our community." The bridge was renamed after Judge S.S. Jolley in 1991, and a second span was added just to its north in 2011. The left photograph shows an aerial view of the Marco River Bridge under construction in the spring of 1969. The photograph below shows a view from atop the bridge looking west towards Marco Island in 1969.

The Marco River Bridge was built by Hardaway Construction Company of Tampa and designed by H.J. Ross Associates of Miami. The project was financed by a Florida Development Commission bond issue and Collier County's secondary gasoline funds. Additionally, the MIDC donated 155,000 yards of fill for the bridge. A 40¢ toll charge was instituted to pay off the construction costs by 1987. Traffic over the bridge exceeded projections, allowing a reduction of the toll from 40¢ to 20¢ in December 1972. The toll was lowered again to 10¢ in 1976 and eliminated altogether in 1979. The photograph above shows the Marco River Bridge nearing completion, as seen from the Marco Island Yacht Club in 1969. The photograph below shows toll gates at the base of the Marco River Bridge in December 1974. (Below, photograph by John Maerker.)

As work began on the Marco River Bridge in 1968, plans were also underway to replace the outdated wooden swing bridge near Goodland. It took seven years for Marco Island's second modern bridge to become a reality. Similar in appearance to the Marco River Bridge, the 1,842-foot span opened on July 30, 1975, as a toll-free bridge. It cost $2.5 million and was built by Cleary Brothers Construction Company of West Palm Beach. The ends of the old wooden trestle bridge were initially left as fishing piers but were later removed. The left photograph shows the Goodland Bridge under construction in 1974, the old swing bridge still operational on its southern (left) side. The photograph below shows the Goodland Bridge, now known as the Stan Gober Memorial Bridge, under construction in late 1974.

Marco Island's most iconic natural landmark is its crescent-shaped beach. The Mackles set aside Residents' Beach for visitors at the end of what is now San Marco Road. Opened in 1965, the 1,000-foot beachfront park was the first on the island to be equipped with parking, restrooms, and refreshment facilities. In 1975, the MIDC deeded the 14.4-acre site to the Marco Island Civic Association (MICA), specifying that the association should maintain the beach for the use and enjoyment of Marco Island residents. In 1980, MICA created the Marco Island Beach Association for the continuing care of the beach and its facilities. The postcard above shows Residents' Beach as it looked in the 1960s. The photograph below shows Residents' Beach on February 27, 1965.

Tigertail Beach is the northernmost public beach on Marco Island. Although a popular destination today, it was once the MIDC's least desirable beachfront due to its lack of accessibility, caused partially by a slough running from the Gulf of Mexico into Clam Bay. In February 1969, the MIDC deeded the land to Collier County as part of a legal obligation to provide public beach access. The long-delayed development of the Tigertail Beach public park began in 1980. The project, which included construction of public facilities and a 300-by-10-foot boardwalk, cost $221,000. The postcard above shows Tigertail Beach sometime after it opened in 1980. The photograph below, taken in 1991, shows the gradual formation of a sandbar, once known as Sand Dollar Island, that eventually connected to Marco Island to create a tidal lagoon at Tigertail Beach. (Below, photograph by Gilbert Booth.)

The southernmost beachfront on Marco Island was once home to a US Air Force missile tracking station and later a concrete mixing plant. Now the site of Cape Marco, the land sold for $14.9 million in 1980, which Frank Mackle Jr. lauded as "another major step in our debt reduction program." This photograph shows the southern end of Marco Island around 1990, prior to the construction of Cape Marco.

Concern over the health of Marco Island's beachfront became a public issue in 1982. A heavy seawall at the former site of the missile tracking station was causing noticeable erosion further up the beach. In response, the Collier County Commissioners established a taxing unit to finance the re-nourishment of the beach in 1988. By February 1991, nearly 40,000 cubic yards of sand had widened the beach by as much as 150 feet.

Coconut Island was a popular uninhabited island off the northwestern coast of Marco Island, near what is now Hideaway Beach. The island was created by Hurricane Donna in 1960, when the southern tip of Sea Oat Island was completely severed, placing the small spit of land just outside of Big Marco Pass. Boaters enjoyed Coconut Island for 45 years until it was completely inundated by Hurricane Wilma's storm surge in 2005, which cut it into two shoals. The photograph above shows Coconut Island on July 8, 1988. The photograph below shows Coconut Island from Hideaway Beach around 1991. (Above, photograph by Smith Aerial Photography, Inc.)

The Marco Island Yacht Club was open for business on January 31, 1965, Deltona's opening day at Marco Island. The $150,000 clubhouse was a social hub, boasting 5,000 square feet of lounge, dining room, kitchen, and meeting space. In addition, the club offered a broad yacht basin with numerous boat slips, a concrete launch ramp, dock, bait and tackle shop, and complete marine gas and oil service. By 1968, the club had over 100 members. The photograph above shows the clubhouse in 1968. The photograph below shows Elliott Mackle speaking at the Marco Island Yacht Club's official dedication on July 4, 1965.

The Marco River Marina opened on February 25, 1967. Catering to an influx of new boaters to Marco Island, the marina included boat sales, rentals, service, protected dockage, hauling, dry storage, fuel, oil, bait and tackle, a launch ramp, showers, and washrooms. Known today as Rose Marina, the boat storage facility underwent major renovations in 2016. The photograph above shows the marina in 1969.

As the population on Marco Island grew, the MIDC made plans to establish a locally owned state-chartered bank. The First National Bank opened on May 14, 1970, as the state's 273rd charter at the corner of North Collier Boulevard and Bald Eagle Drive. At the close of the first day of business, the bank's total footings exceeded $1 million. The photograph above shows the bank in May 1970.

In September 1980, the Marco Island Chamber of Commerce purchased a $40,000 passenger trolley to provide public transportation to visitors. The trolley took its inaugural trip on November 30, 1980, charging 25¢ per ride. The trolley was named *Mar-Go*, a winning contest entry submitted by community leader M. Jane Hittler. The photograph above shows the trolley in front of the Marriott's Marco Beach Hotel around 1980.

The *Rosie O'Shea* was an authentic 104-foot paddle wheel boat purchased by Bill Rose in May 1985 for use at O'Shea's Restaurant on Marco Island, which was owned by Tom and Dolores Shea. Constructed in Racine, Wisconsin, the boat accommodated 150 passengers and featured two decks, a dining room, two cocktail lounges, and a dance floor. The boat operated until 1998. The photograph above shows the *Rosie O'Shea* in November 1986.

Marco Island's first shopping center opened in July 1965, offering access to a barbershop and beauty salon, hardware store, 7-Eleven supermarket, and service station. Less than a year later, the center underwent an expansion due to the volume of business it received. This photograph shows the post office (left), which opened in November 1965, and shopping center in 1967.

A second shopping center opened on June 19, 1969, providing an additional 25,000 square feet of shopping space. The largest new tenant was a Winn-Dixie supermarket, shown above in a 1968 rendering. The plaza was marketed as the first "one of everything" facility for residents of Marco Island and the surrounding area. Today, it is known as the Marco Town Center Mall, and a Publix supermarket has replaced the original Winn-Dixie.

Five

THEN AND NOW

John Maerker (1920–2014) had a keen photographic eye and the terrific foresight to capture the growth and development of Marco Island with his camera. For 15 years, between 1965 and 1980, Maerker created dozens of photographic slides, which he routinely and enthusiastically presented to audiences in his living room. The authors hope to honor Maerker's legacy by literally following in his footsteps to share his photographs alongside modern comparisons.

John Maerker found Marco Island in 1965 through a promotional slideshow by a Deltona salesman at Sanibel Island, Florida. Following the presentation, John and his wife, Mary, bought a lot on Marco Island near Tigertail Beach—years before the area was scheduled to be developed. The photograph above shows Mary Maerker (left) and son standing on their purchased lot on Henderson Court in December 1971. Their house was built in 1973 and for some time had unobstructed views of the Gulf of Mexico. The photograph below shows the Maerker house on Henderson Court on February 16, 2018. (Above, photograph by John Maerker; below, photograph by Austin Bell.)

The photograph above shows another view of the Maerkers' lot on Henderson Court in December 1971, with Mary Maerker standing in the "backyard." The Maerkers had direct access to this waterway, which connects to Collier Bay and, ultimately, the Gulf of Mexico. The spot where John was standing while taking this photograph would later be replaced by a bridge to open the waterway further south. Spinnaker Drive is on the left, and Henderson Court is on the right. The February 16, 2018, photograph below shows the same view but from the Blackmore Court bridge with houses lining the waterway. (Above, photograph by John Maerker; below, photograph by Austin Bell.)

Maerker captured a series of photographs in December 1974 that showcase the streets and views he encountered on the way to his Henderson Court house. The first photograph he shot after coming onto the island was at the intersection of North Collier Boulevard and Bald Eagle Drive (above). Compared to the bustling intersection today (seen below on March 30, 2018), the quiet streets included only directional signs on the right and the First Bank of Marco Island on the left. Today, this is the busiest intersection on Marco Island and is one of its primary centers of business and commerce. (Above, photograph by John Maerker; below, photograph by Austin Bell.)

In December 1974, Maerker took the photograph above of the Collier Boulevard bridge over Smokehouse Bay. Built in the late 1960s, the bridge further aided the development of Marco Island by connecting Smokehouse Bay to inland waterways. After years of discussion, the bridge was completely rebuilt between 2014 and 2015 at the cost of more than $8 million. In 2015, the City of Marco Island renamed the bridge in honor of Deltona architect and longtime resident Herbert R. Savage, with a formal dedication on May 30, 2016. The February 16, 2018, photograph below shows the Herbert R. Savage Bridge adjacent to the Esplanade (right), which houses shops, residences, and a marina. (Above, photograph by John Maerker; below, photograph by Austin Bell.)

Turning left from Tigertail Court and heading west on Hernando Drive, Maerker reached its intersection with Spinnaker Drive. The photograph above, taken in December 1974, shows the natural vegetation preventing access to what eventually became Tigertail Beach. In 1964, the Marco Island Development Corporation gifted 28 acres of land to Collier County for the beach, but at that time, it was only accessible from the then-undeveloped east. The photograph below shows the same intersection on April 4, 2018. Hernando Drive now extends west and includes Tigertail Beach public access, parking lot, and facilities. (Above, photograph by John Maerker; below, photograph by Austin Bell.)

Residential bridges, like the one in these photographs, were built as part of Deltona's master plan to construct hundreds of miles of waterways. Opening new waterways meant more waterfront homes and greater boating access. The photograph above shows a newly completed bridge on Hernando Drive in June 1979. The photograph below shows the same bridge on April 4, 2018. (Above, photograph by John Maerker; below, photograph by Austin Bell.)

Before the Marco River Bridge opened in 1969, the only vehicular bridge to Marco Island was a wooden trestle bridge with a swing span near Goodland. A 55-foot-high, 1,842-foot-long bridge replaced the swing bridge on July 30, 1975. In 2013, the bridge, formerly known as the Goodland Bridge, was renamed the Stan Gober Memorial Bridge in honor of 40-year Goodland resident Stan Gober (1926–2012). Gober, the founder and owner of Stan's Idle Hour, was honored for his impact on the community and his work on behalf of numerous charitable causes. The photograph above was taken in June 1976, less than a year after the new bridge opened. The photograph below shows the same bridge 42 years later on February 16, 2018. (Above, photograph by John Maerker; below, photograph by Austin Bell.)

In April 1975, Maerker photographed Marco Island from atop the Marco River Bridge looking west (above). Visible in this photograph are the Marco Island Yacht Club (foreground), Sunset House North, Sunset House, Emerald Beach, and Tradewinds beachfront condominiums (extreme background), and numerous residential homes. The photograph below was taken from atop the newer bridge spanning the Marco River (constructed in 2011), now the S.S. Jolley Bridge, on March 30, 2018. The four beachfront condominiums (background) are still in view compared to the 1975 photograph, but new buildings, including at the yacht club (foreground), dwarf the original structures. The authors would like to note that the risks associated with taking such a photograph have decreased since Maerker took his, thanks largely to the addition of protective sidewalks to the 2011 bridge span. (Above, photograph by John Maerker; below, photograph by Austin Bell.)

The first shopping center on Marco Island was completed by July 1965 and housed a barbershop, beauty salon, dry cleaner, hardware store, and 7-Eleven. Growth over the next year led to store expansions. Tudor Jones, owner of the hardware store, saw a 200-percent increase in sales between November 1965 and October 1966, while the 7-Eleven reported that "our volume is as great as some older, established stores of our chain in Fort Myers." The hardware store is now occupied by various tenants, and the 7-Eleven is now Kretch's Restaurant. The photograph above shows the shopping center in May 1968. The photograph below shows the building almost 50 years later, on February 16, 2018. (Above, photograph by John Maerker; below, photograph by Austin Bell.)

Marco Island's second modern post office opened in November 1965. Replacing the post office in Old Marco, Elliott Mackle noted that the erection of a new post office was "an indication of the rapid growth which the Marco Island community has experienced since its inauguration last winter [January 1965]." The Bermuda-style building was "designed to represent the . . . architectural style predominant in the community." By August 1966, postmaster Max Scott noted a 400-percent increase in mail volume, a 250-percent increase in postal receipts, and a staff increase to three full-time employees. The building has since been converted into a restaurant (Su's Garden). The photograph above shows the post office in May 1968, complete with a telephone booth. The photograph below shows the building on February 16, 2018, surrounded by other commercial buildings. (Above, photograph by John Maerker; below, photograph by Austin Bell.)

John Maerker visited Marco Island's first beachfront condominium, Emerald Beach, in October 1966. Less than a year old at the time, the seven-story building was a huge milestone for Deltona in its master plan for the island, the first of many high-rise beachfront condominiums. Taking the photograph above from the water, Maerker was also able to capture a rainbow in the frame. Over 50 years later, Emerald Beach still stands, but everything beyond the condominium has changed. The beach has been drastically expanded through re-nourishment projects, changing what was once a short walk from the condo to the Gulf of Mexico into a significant hike. Pictured below on April 4, 2018, the Emerald Beach is now crowded between Tradewinds (right), Sunset House, and Sunset House North condominiums. (Above, photograph by John Maerker; below, photograph by Austin Bell.)

Aside from traveling in an aircraft, the best aerial views of Marco Island in the later 1960s were from the rooftop of the seven-story Emerald Beach condominium. Looking east in June 1966, Maerker saw a sparse island with unpaved roads and five houses located around Greenbrier Street, Manor Terrace, Buttercup Court, Wintergreen Court, and Dandelion Court (above). The same view is nearly unrecognizable today, as seen below on March 30, 2018, with several condominium complexes in the foreground and development extending much farther east, almost as far as the eye can see. (Above, photograph by John Maerker; below, photograph by Austin Bell.)

Although it still bears its trademark crescent shape, Marco Island's famous beachfront has probably seen more development than any other part of the island during the past 50 years. Both of these photographs were taken from the roof of the Emerald Beach Condominium, the one above in June 1966 and the one below on March 30, 2018. The most conspicuous difference is the density of beachfront buildings, many more of which are obscured by the Tradewinds building in the foreground (left below). The only other buildings along the beach in June 1966 were the Marco Beach Hotel (center above) and remnants of the missile tracking station on the extreme southern point. A substantial widening of the beach is also noticeable, thanks largely to a beach restoration in 1990 and other re-nourishment projects to combat erosion in the years since. (Above, photograph by John Maerker; below, photograph by Austin Bell.)

Six

WE ARE MARCO

The Mackle brothers may have laid the foundation for what is now the city of Marco Island, but it is the people who call it home that have shaped its modern identity. Today, Marco Island is an active and vibrant community, steeped in history, generous in spirit, and surprisingly close-knit. People are proud to live on Marco Island, and that same pride has forged a special sense of community.

There are dozens of active community groups on Marco Island, many of which have been making a difference for decades. The Marco Island Woman's Club was founded in 1966 and has undertaken countless projects designed to improve community services and facilities while promoting sociability. The club founded the first Marco Island Library in October 1968 (above). M. Jane Hittler, Bernice Newton, and June Murphy formed the nonprofit Marco Youth Center, Inc., in 1973 to unite the community behind the idea that the local youth needed more to do on the island. The photograph below shows M. Jane Hittler (left), Bernice Newton, and Elliot Fisher (right) at the future site of the Marco Youth Center in April 1974. In 1977, the Marco Youth Center effectively became the Marco Island YMCA.

Fire and police departments were established early on to serve Marco Island's rapidly growing population. Both divisions worked hard to keep the community safe and did so with the help of island residents. The island's first fire station was dedicated on February 1, 1969, along with a demonstration of the new LaFrance fire engine (above). Aside from a chief and assistant chief, the fire department was staffed by dedicated community volunteers who completed comprehensive training. Les Binns (below, pictured with police dog Fuzz) was the island's first full-time deputy sheriff. He was assigned to Marco Island in the summer of 1966. Binns said that his primary duty in his new assignment was "to keep people happy." Initially on his own, Binns came to rely on residents to help keep an eye on the developing community.

Marco Island's first newspaper, the *Marco Island Eagle*, published its inaugural eight-page issue on March 31, 1968. Passionate community members William Tamplin (1918–1982, left), Raymond Henle (right), and Jane Hamlin established the newspaper themselves, dedicating it "to the best interests of the people who have invested their money here and have chosen this beautiful area for their homes and, in many cases, to make their livelihood." The *Marco Eagle* is still in print, now a subsidiary of the *Naples Daily News*.

```
RECOUNTED 9/3/97
4:46 P.M.
                    GENERAL ELECTION - COLLIER COUNTY, FLORIDA
                              AUGUST 28, 1997                            PAGE   1
    Summary Report: Final Report                    PRECINCT            COUNTY
                                                 TOTAL  PERCENT      TOTAL  PERCENT

    TOTAL PRECINCTS                                                      7
    PRECINCTS COUNTED                                                    7    100. 00

    TOTAL REGISTERED VOTERS                                           8932
    TOTAL VALID BALLOTS                                               6301     70. 54
    TOTAL BALLOTS                                                     6301     70. 54

    INCORPORATION OF THE CITY  OF MARCO ISLAND ** VF 1
         YES                                    # .222.                3133     51. 49
         NO                                     # .224.                2952     48. 51
```

One of the most influential community movements came when residents voted to incorporate Marco Island. After several failed attempts in the 1980s, Marco Island officially became a city on August 28, 1997. Passing by merely 181 votes, the incorporation symbolized a new chapter for Marco Island and its residents.

In August 1983, the Deltona Corporation presented Collier County with the deed to 29 acres in the middle of Marco Island for use as a public park. The park was dedicated in Frank Mackle Jr.'s name on June 4, 1987, and has been a staple in the community ever since. The photograph above shows Mackle cutting the ribbon at Frank E. Mackle Jr. Park. (Photograph by Frances M. Stahl, courtesy of the *Marco Eagle*.)

Since its founding in 1994, the Marco Island Historical Society had ambitions to build a history museum on Marco Island. After 16 years of temporary museums at different locations around the island (right), the MIHS partnered with Collier County to build the Marco Island Historical Museum in 2010. Today, the award-winning museum welcomes 25,000 visitors annually.

Marco Island has seen its share of devastating hurricanes throughout the past half-century. On August 24, 1992, Hurricane Andrew battered Marco Island with 100-mile-per-hour winds, leaving millions of dollars in property damage in its wake. Thirteen years later, on October 24, 2005, Hurricane Wilma made landfall just south of Marco Island at Cape Romano, with sustained winds reaching 120 miles per hour. And on September 10, 2017, fifty-seven years to the day after it was decimated by Hurricane Donna, Marco Island bore the full brunt of Hurricane Irma's 130-mile-per-hour winds and storm surge. The photograph above shows the view from M. Jane Hittler Park on Marco Island during Hurricane Andrew. The photograph below shows the historic Capt. John F. Horr house in September 2017, heavily damaged by Hurricane Irma. (Above, photograph by Astrid Rincon, courtesy of the *Marco Eagle*; below, photograph by Joey Waves.)

Even in the wake of some the most infamous hurricanes in US history, Marco Islanders have rallied together to rebuild and carry on. During Hurricane Irma, a group of caring volunteer civilians known as the Marco Patriots provided critical information, supplies, and assistance to those who chose to ride it out. After the storm, they provided critical information and updates to evacuated residents, still displaced and anxious to learn the fates of their homes and businesses. The Marco Patriots eventually raised nearly $150,000 to aid hurricane relief in Marco Island and its heavily impacted neighbors in Everglades City, Goodland, and Naples. The photograph above shows the remnants of a carport at the Essex on Marco Island on September 15, 2017. The photograph below shows, from left to right, Erin Wolfe Bell, Colleen Popoff, Michelle Sturzenegger, Theresa Gantner, Lar Sturzenegger, and Rob Popoff, who volunteered to clean up the Marco Island Cemetery on September 17, 2017. (Photographs by Austin Bell.)

Visit us at
arcadiapublishing.com

Printed in the USA
CPSIA information can be obtained
at www.ICGtesting.com
LVHW082303121123
763743LV00007B/78